The Book of Open Secrets

By Aayushi Tripathi

To Yohana,
For calling me relentlessly.

<u>***Prologue***</u>

In the pages of this book lie a gathering of poems
birthed from experimentation, life's tapestry, and an
unwavering passion for the beauty of language. It is my
humble offering to those whose essence has sparked the
ink to flow, immortalizing the myriad of human
experiences in verse.

Within its four sections, I extend to each reader a
chance to delve into the depths of introspection, to stir
dormant emotions, and perhaps, to embolden the spirit
towards novel paths in life.

ONE FOR THE WORLD

Language

To me,
Language is more than just words.
A part of the song just before the chorus interrupts.

A fragment of mind forming arms and feet,
To walk, if not run to build its destiny.
It's wondrous to advocate how,
The pace of your breath and rhythm of your heart,
Speaks louder than your warming jaw,
Being more transparent and breve even before,
Your mind reverts with its malicious and conceded art.

To me,
Language is an obsession.
A part of the play just before tragedy erupts.

Destructive as it may have been portrayed,
It lingers still waiting for the silence to be broken,
A nod, a hug, a peck or even vocal disarray.
It breeds in your stew, so stew carefully in your stay,
Sometimes words are better left unattended,
A sentence your breath will convey.

<u>*A Disease Called Time*</u>

Looks like you've figured it out,
Lingering feelings and a faint heart.
To ache for love and not to love for ache,
A seemingly justified art.

Feels like you've plotted the turnabout,
Festering wounds to avoid a new start.
You could have told him everything by the lake,
Things that are truly ripping you apart.

Express when you are bound and bowed,
A trend that us children were impart.
Now watch us wipe the tears with a rake,
And console a beating jar with a dart.

Only if someone told you about limit,
How limited times these limitless breathes chime,
After all we are all sick and dying,
Dying of a disease called Time.

<u>***Price for Insecurity***</u>

Love is lost in the wake of the new world,
'Forever with one' rescued no one from the trap,
That was nestled to stop insecurity from irritating
momentum,
Just to escape having the truth look at your future in
mishap.

The insecurity crept onto the tired and restless,
To limit and shame the bonds we were weaving
alongside them,
The maiden who could never love in mistrust,
Turned every other person against this powerful realm.

The fair one elected monogamy as the new ruler,
To deceive and guilt others to trap themselves in her
hunger,
She couldn't bear to stand the sight,
That her chosen one could also connect well with
others.
And that's when we lost love.
The intent of us was to share and care,
Demanding association of different kinds of love,
Let it be those coffee dates or jogger's in warfare,
Each one requires the freedom to choose its own
messenger in the form of a dove.

The bonds are independent just like with the one you
end up,
But each commands privacy for the minds and hearts to
intersect.
The carnal one you select to be yours and theirs,
And then there's others you choose with the new names
you elect.

In the roles of customary proprietors in the estate of
love,
Touch became threatening and distance became novelty
currency,
Hugs were libidinized to an extent until,
We lost our roots to being humans who are now
voyaging for eternity.
A gallantry to the maiden for the price she put on
insecurity.

<u>Sixth Sense</u>

What is sixth sense I wondered?
And in all the versions I found,
The answer was never rendered,
So, finally I stopped asking around,
To allow myself to completely surrender.

But I noticed because that's a job I am meant to attend
to,
I noticed how I attested,
My thoughts and patterns on the days I rue,
Because my senses are heightened,
Only to realize my best audience has always been you.

With you, I could feel without touch,
Hear without words,
See without actions,
Smell in your absence,
And taste different flavors of your mood.

Suddenly it was right there standing all tough,
The name they couldn't anoint,
Because it takes a little more than just some buzz,
It has a lot more to do with a sense not everyone can
appoint,
I believe sixth sense is nothing but love.

<u>***Overwhelm until Consumption or
Consumption until Overwhelm?***</u>

She only knew how to strangle herself,
But the intense heat of the burning emotion,
Set her on a path of pressuring aggression,
Until she couldn't strangle so she lit herself on fire on
her very own hearth,
In an attempt that a new her comes to surface
surrendering.

In the twilight of a new day,
The blood rushed backwards,
Thicker, more claret than red,
For the blaze intensified the blood,
Introducing a darker, fearless red head.
Her bones cracked,
Each one had gone under obliteration,
For her to be reborn,
She must forget what broke her the first time,
And why her malleable bones needed permanence.

She rose,
And she rose like nothing changed,
Except everything had changed,
Her direction, intention, and priority,
The town knew who she WAS,
But couldn't remember,
Who SHE was indeed.

Overwhelm until consumption is not equivalent,
To consumption until overwhelm,
Some steps are late but better late than never,
Allow your overwhelm to defeat its purpose,
Some overwhelm burn you instead,

For new blood and bones,
You must burn first.

Envoys of Illiteracy

Lurked in the silence,
He stood taller than his rising height,
A mind bestowed to the pages written in history,
He became obsessed with adding his name to the
book of the might.

The world had order,
And the ranks were not his strongest suit,
He preferred gallivanting the darker corners,
Earning gallantry for his own history in pursuit.

He spoke of literary and works of writers he revered,
The tradition of norm was replaced by Science,
And of numbers he sketched his mind into a palace of
his own,
He reached the darkness in the times of folklore and
the naive.

Gathered were the townspeople in the debacle of his
work,
The crimes he committed had to be addressed in front
of all,
The elders knew what comes of literacy and he who
literates,
Must be silenced for the order to be restored.

The man who wanted to be in the pages of history,
Known as the envoy against illiteracy,
Ceased up in the pages recording illicit advocacy,
For committing the crime to have had a thought.

Dichotomy

In a few rumbles and thunders,
Struck some wonders in the blunders,
The nightmare of a sultry hunter,
A lion disguised as a deer waiting in hunger.

In a few rumbles and thunders,
Struck some wonders in the blunders,
Twitching every nerve in the construct,
That is love in this belittling contest of winners.

In a few rumbles and thunders,
Struck some wonders in the blunders,
Every damsel is schooled to be her own knight in
shining armor,
But is preferred by every knight invoking the inner
coward.

In a few rumbles and thunders,
Struck some wonders in the blunders,
Whether it's your mother, brother, or lover,
Everyone can turn into another festering monger.

In a few rumbles and thunders,
Struck some wonders in the blunders,
Life eases into winter after summer,
Like nothing happened and not a word was ever uttered.

<u>*I have the Strangest Feeling*</u>

I've got the strangest feeling.
Dusk came quick and decided to stay around.

Time is turning into moments,
Past and future are now and near,
Fragments shall remain of what manages to become,
A core, not just a mere memory in a tense that's lived,
A thousand fragments that were beyond just surreal.

Sleep is turning into reflection of what we bear,
So as to forfeit what couldn't withstand the alignment,
For all that exists will manifest every thought into
existence,
Nonetheless of your want or need of confinement,
Let the mind retweet the bitter design of the world that
defines us.

Life is a rhythmic repetition of breathing,
I assumed the power to the mind that's controlling the
breath,
But would you call the ocean more powerful,
Simply because you witness the tantrum like it's the
hoarder of death,
Or would you grace the moon for the tides he rides to
watch the calm in the disappeared nights?

Options have become choices,
To limit the internalizing patterns of habit,
A choice as limited as it may sound to the average of
them around,
It is the ultimate deal of all the options that open in the
gambit,
Of life when choices are molded to govern discipline

that's profound.

I discovered the strangest dawn,
In the wake of the few that surround.

God's Drifted Dog

She saw God when he knocked on her door,
Teary eyed, she began collecting everything she
owns,
Dusted distant memories and packed them into a
translucent travel sized bag,
While it played in the background, she felt comfort
and terror in her bones.

One by one, she packed all she acquired in her life,
Including her unboxed passion and a taste she never
really owned,
She watched her memories being distorted in her
plain sight,
And how she lost the key to her magical door.

And so, she broke down when things got clearer,
To have stricken with answers that were timeworn,
Yet she finally felt happy that her blindfold was
indeed a blindfold,
A piece of cloth that was the last thing she needed
to mourn.

She turned to god with her luggage and some rosy
nose,
To have felt pretty before the divine was like a
parting gift bestowed,
She took a deep breath but started to weep some
more,
I guess she wasn't ready to leave this way especially
after all that was disclosed.

God looked at her with not a twitch on his forehead,
He watched her break the silence before him and the
hour,

She told him all that she wanted but couldn't get,
Because all she ever wanted was love and depended
on others.

She spoke of her woes and her struggles of implore,
And as she spoke, she began patting her days that
were old,
She for once celebrated the person she became
fighting against the person,
She could have become if she didn't silently fight
that battle all alone.

And as she stood in front of god,
She felt loved without another in the shadow,
Astonished at how it felt for she waited to feel this
her whole life,
Her tear shifted to another emotion; a feeling of
peace overflowed.

She rejoiced in his presence,
And let him watch her madness break the bounds,
She could love and feel love and it was his presence
to which she owed,
So, she thanked him and reluctantly, she was ready
to submit herself to him if that's what he sought.

She held her luggage tightly and whispered not so
slow,
"You can't miss a sign from the universe,
It keeps getting louder and louder till you respond.
But I didn't expect to see you come downtown into
my home."

God looked at her in question and perplexity,
"Why is my visit assumed with intentions of
reaping the unlisted?"

She found herself befuddled in serenity,
God replied "I was just looking for my dog that
drifted".

<u>***Reality***</u>

The mind is a fickle friend,
It thinks and scripts waiting to be scripted, indeed.
However, it's the days when I can't hold my pen,
That speaks more to me than when I hold it,
nevertheless

Because if I write, it becomes a reality.
Unfolding the blindfold, I'm not willing to free.
If I let it float in my head, it remains the truth,
A truth untold but a truth nevertheless.

For a truth is conveying a rising sun,
Offset a progressing cold, dark dusk.
A reality is the sun at large above the horizon,
8 minutes late but at large nevertheless.

However, it's fated to confuse so to profuse,
A truth can't exist without reality,
A reality consists of multiple truths,
A dusk, the sun, a plane and the living or surviving
nevertheless.

So, while forging your multiple truths,
You may lose control but you can keep creating,
More truth to favor your ending,
Because a reality will exist, nevertheless.

Fall is Lurking

The chill in autumn breeze,
The tank of gas that' s stained with grease,
Shuddering are the ones who find it hard,
To accept the precarious state of this art.

The fall of the first leaf,
The dawn or dusk nearly oblique.
Smell the air as it passes you by,
This time of the year tastes like a bottle of rye.

The world dresses,
As the nature undresses.
Then marches to match
The rhythm that caresses.

September to October,
And then Mid to November,
Could it all be devised
For the halt that's taking over.

The Earth drenched,
Seeping and soaking,
I smelled the air,
The fall is lurking!

<u>*He Lastly Whispered*</u>

Time was soaring and staring,
Syncing with the wind that was gusting and whistling
the past,
Teasing the breathing and calming the dying,
I closed my eyes thanking every second that last,
Watching the undead with every hour they were
tricking.

The wait for the night to be over superseded,
Every secondary thought like peace.
However, the number of injured and wounded
exceeded,
Recording the ugliest battle of armor and grease.
Locking a mental image of the bloodbath that couldn't
be deleted.

Rushed, as I stumbled upon one such lad,
Losing his life for the higher honor of country and
might.
Stitches, bandages, and gauges were all I had,
That could support him in his invincible second fight.
He fought well but not better than the battle ground,
might I add.

He was young and with such youth he could offer,
A country, the civilian it deserved.
But I watched him loose his youth before her,
The woman who had longed for her future that couldn't
be conserved,
Knowing she said her goodbyes when he left her
amongst strangers.

I tried to save what was left of him,
But he knew that tomorrow only his memories would

be unearthed.
He looked in my eyes with peace and a whim,
Watching death standing by his bed and as it lingered,
He let out his last words without any grim,
"You are beautiful", he lastly whispered.

The story

Some stories begin to end perfectly.
Some stories end to define a new beginning.
While some just teach that's it's okay to pause,
And offer yourself to live every moment that's
occurring.

One such story that pauses time,
Takes only a few words but leaves plenty behind
Is the story of a fish in her prime,
In the marine that's ruthless, may I remind.

She dreamt of finding the ocean one day,
And swim her way to the perfect life.
She met an older fish on her way to find,
Wondered if she would find the answer that would
make her feel more alive.

"Where is the ocean", questioned the juvenile,
"This is the ocean.", answered the older fish with a
smile.
 "What? This is water. What I want is the ocean."
She found herself stricken with reality that eased her
after a while.

The Witch of Salem

The girl on the far, far side of the track,
Lived alone above an arcade up the alley,
With hooded eyes so bad, rad like no turning back,
From the life she chose as the modern witch in the
valley,
Of Salem rising for an attack.

The nearest of dear is still farther from her reach,
She killed the man who is remembered as,
The jewel of Salem who woke the town with his
palpable screech.
Dared not one to stumble across or in sight with she
that has,
No moral compass to point the magnetic north to her
southern diabolic preach.

Come dusk time, she wanders around the witches town,
Scathing each track to prowling every corner,
For those with the whim in the whitest of gown,
Who have been sniffing the innocent and festering on
the loner.
The man she killed was one such dreadful clown.

It's funny how Salem has solemnly scarred,
The girl who believed in medicine, art, botany and
some stars,
If anything its historic and profoundly carved,
In the pages of history that Salem was always at war,
With purest of hearts going over and beyond
superstition so grimly scarfed.

<u>***Womb-man***</u>

The glory of revolution, knitting, baking after
evolution,
The hands were only controlling a fleet of emotion,
When they are capable of holding tools and weapons of
destruction.

Eons, Eras, Periods, Epochs and Ages,
Freedom, Voice, Feminism and Wages.
"Forth thou March" to "Break the Cages",
She began to strive in all of those pages.

Turned the tables when she was furious
Of Slavery, abduction, rape and "Save us".
I suggest you to be cautious,
For the day when she finally stops being anxious.

Her journey starts as early as a rooster of a cock in the
morning.
She educates herself in the hope of finding,
A life that's worth combing, dressing, feeding, and
loving.
And when she rests from her early struggles
anticipating,
Life has different plans and she has no idea what's
coming.

Prepared to change from jewelry to diapers,
Daughters, Wives, Colleagues and Mothers.
Wiping tears to molding characters,
She is the true gold to all the treasurers.

Out of all that she is known as,
Being a mother will she never pass,
She is the only teacher in your ungeared class,

Hell bent to turn you into a sass.

One day it will all be worth it.
Your efforts and dedication will certainly fit.
On my path, to the ground should I hit,
Pull me up and help me remember my bit.

This day cannot begin to stack,
Everything I want to give that you lack,
Although to my best ability present in my sack,
Is this poem written in black.

<u>***Safety Net***</u>

Have you ever jumped off into the sunset without a
safety net?

The world is so much easier to take a dive when you
know there's someone in a cloak,
To catch you or guard you or revive you,
When nothing else has the potential to regain you.
It's easier to take the stairs when there's a stop you
know is hatched on low,
To relax or breathe or just take a minute to wash that
annihilating blue,
Or just simply to banter the existential woes.

But what about the people who don't have a hand to
hold?
Have you seen them jump before they're too old?
I guess the other hand wasn't just for you to clap at
those rescuing the folklore,
Sometimes you have to be the one who picks, revives,
and holds your own jittery mittens on the sullen road.

Those are the people with the potential to make life,
A sultry surprise with a touch of originality that's
always ready to take a dive.
These people are built different and how wonderful it is
to watch them strive,
For they have missed the sunset so many times before,
But the missed sunset brought them the midnight to
drive them into a new morning light,
With the sunrise they grow because that's how you
really fold.

<u>*Heaven*</u>

Heaven exists.
At least to me.
Let me paint you a picture,
Paradise in three.

Remember cosmos?
The space that's ceaseless,
Perpetually demanding,
Incessantly inevitable,
Clasps a distinct body.
Remember Moon?
Freezing and distant,
Like an exile cast into darkness.
It's marvelous how yet
It shines the hardest.
With me yet?
Go to a beach.
Not for the sea.
Let it unfold the majestic,
Phenomenon of paramount degree.
Watch how something so far away,
Dictate something so profoundly laid.
The ocean, my friend, is an endless braid.
Hanging on the back of this world,
A twirling whirlpool that's swirling away.

You're telling me it's that simple?
To command the relentless and hungry body that is
water?
Its shallow and furious,
Tempestuous and variable
Yet dances high and low,
On the force that is audacious.

It's beautiful simply,
To imagine that
A human so tiny
Can witness such a statuesque wonder
Of the many wonders the cosmos beholds
By breathing endlessly.

How can you say heaven doesn't exist?

The Dragon's Cocoon

'Oh, how wonderful it would be if she left!'
Whispered the townspeople with a blister in their
intents,
She was born a chirp-less bird to a cooing nightingale
of the soaring manor,
She was never to aim higher than a dropping feather,
Cocooned as an infant, remained inside through her
youth shielding her honor.

Soon the cocoon couldn't fit her to keep her warm,
So she started to spread one wing at a time,
Every turbulence through her wing would encourage
the laughter,
Her wings would flutter and bring out the jitters to stop
her,
Only to go back crawling inside to cry but she would
try again soon after.

Sometimes the wings are tougher to spread,
She tried to control but the wings couldn't take that first
flight,
In her frustration people saw an opportunity to poke
again,
She cried but couldn't go back inside because her home
couldn't fit her,
She felt betrayed to have no place in the world that
turned out to be so inhumane.

The creature that couldn't fly was now even homeless,
She started to hear the remarks they brewed in the
market,
And dragged her tiresome wings searching for a place
to bury herself for the night,

Until she realized that there was no difference left,
Between the suffocation she felt inside the cocoon or
under this moonlight.
And suddenly there was not a home left for her to hide.
Helpless, hopeless, and heedless she began to rummage
through the empty streets,
And in an attempt to escape her embarrassment,
She ran harder than life for life has been running away
from that nurturing sunlight,
Darting through the emotions she sprinted all teary,
And chucked her wings so hard to despise her burden
that took off as her first flight.

She floated through the crispy winds of the colder
nights for about ten seconds,
But those ten seconds gave her the most important
lesson of her life,
While she was trying to takeoff one wing at a time
because it was too heavy,
What she assumed to be her biggest baggage is actually
meant,
To help a dragon soar up higher than plane even if
some consider it beastly.

Oh, how wonderful it was that she felt,
For in her feelings, she created the beast she was born
to be,
Those she scares are one winged flyer,

  And those brave enough, find a cocoon in her,
Because home is a person not a place where you are not
a suffocating survivor.

<u>***Anonymity***</u>

Is it just me or?
Are you also stuck?
In the dimensional construct of class,
And some inspirational junk?

The generational trauma,
Roaring higher than mediocre luck.
Trauma is made up,
An excuse for you to be stuck up.

Choose to let go of this
Woke dream of cleaning the rut.
Wake up to accept one day,
One time and one moment,
Of your not-so-mightier self-cut up.

Nothing is impossible;
Somethings are improbable;
It will become more plausible,
When you realize everything is evincible.

There's so much to do,
There's so much to be,
Just befriend the anonymity.

<u>*A Walk Not So Alone*</u>

Learn to accept that there's no one to walk with you
forever but you, they said.
I saw so many broken hearts and crushed souls agreeing
to that juvenile sentiment.
And all I want to do is ask,
Ask every man and woman to remember the time,
When we marched to freedom, together.
When we painted the brighter future, together.
When we danced next to that bonfire, together;
together.

Togetherness can never be found if you are just looking
to,
Cage it. Date it. Marry it. Bound it.
To keep it locked just for you forever.

We are teaching each other to love oneself,
But do not tell the difference between love and greed.
And as we watch narcissism being birthed right
amongst,
We watch and watch and keep on watching the brute
we freed.

"We are sick of artificial"
"Everything is fake"
So please justify why you trust more the intelligence
that is artificial,
And a reality that is fake.

Yes, we are the victim.
But we are also to blame.
Once you stop acting victimized,
We can change the game.

People are meant for people.
Do not learn to accept that there's no one to walk with
you forever but you.
There's going to be so many wonderful hands to hold as
you walk,
Just allow yourself to believe it to be true.
Because it is.
Look around you.

It's your Choice

There're two forms of "it's your choice",
One that accompanies manipulation.
Is it though? Our choice?
Why does it feel like everything else but our real
intention?

A choice today is not as independent as liberty is being
sold,
If we could truly choose,
It would all end up in shambles much likely to cause
chaos,
Because every choice would befit only you.

It's not really your choice.
Every choice is a business with numbers calculated,
You either close this deal with profit,
Or lose it by paying in exhaustion and feeling
inadequate.

And then there's another form of "it's your choice",
That accompanies an invitation.
Would it be so inconvenient for you to instead say?
"I would love it if you do", in the end?

Being terrified of vulnerability or rejection,
Charted our direction to distance,
In the hope that eventually no one could break in,
Or see us bare in the act of this conditional resistance.

Regardless of the origin of this invention,
It's just pointless in plain view,
To continue to support this idea of suggestion,
It's okay to care and comfort without turning things
blue.

<u>Femininity</u>

A sense of tranquility,
Manifests itself as energy.
The kind of energy,
That turns you weak in the knee,
While turning your will into potential and then
eventually,
A reality.

That's divine feminine.

If you find yourself,
Surrounded by men with languid masculinity,
You're weak in your femininity.
Because the power of womanhood,
Is an inevitable magnet to a man,
That can match this energy.

The answer was always within,
Because the within is another universe,
To which the one outside must sync.
Find what's blocking your feminine,
From shining so bright that it attracts,
Only those who can see in the sun without any sting.

The Twin

What a pinnacle of species are men,
Paraded as reapers of women,
But the ultimate protectors are also them.
In the midst of fiasco, we might forget,
To appreciate the pioneers that are men.

Have you had the privilege to watch a man be him?
In his natural form and from the rawness within,
His nerves are always twitching,
To set his creator's side wild and rampant,
And build a foundation for the world we live in.

In the ranks of the butch, the jocks and the classier akin,
There exists a poet, an artist, and a racer deep in their
skin,
And for some, aimless as he may have been,
It's just one lesser aim to be truly free to begin.

The seekers of the world, if you will,
Watch them in love and how far they swim,
The world isn't enough to adore,
Their patience, will and depth of,
Their lover's instinct.

As marvelous are their roles herein,
Oh, the wonder has the lovers been,
No matter how much you hate them,
Man was created for woman,
As their soul's twin.

<u>*Roads*</u>

Sometimes, a road is not the correct pathway for
everyone,
In rare times, not all walk on a lane in search of the
highway,
For those scarce times, you bump into people that were
given planes to fly,
And the hardest times are for those who keep trying to
fit into lanes that were meant to be walked.

The actual path of a plane is never on the road,
A runway is only useful for the ascent of the abode,
And returns after the journey is over for the final
descent,
It's the uncharted ground against gravity that must be
navigated to truly understand the potential it bore.

The roads that fit so well for others are for the vehicles
they're carrying,
Every transport is designed to fulfil its own journey,
And each has its own fun whether you're cruising
through the winds on the road,
Or the ship that sails in the winds of their own,
The same wind blows differently for everyone to who it
owes.

<u>An Irony</u>

Truer than real,
A glimpse of all that pervades.
Must sanity be sanctioned,
By a murder of crows?
While the dolphins are busy knitting,
The unlit part of their brains.

Ironic than unusual,
The state of affairs in this place.
They fight with love, for love,
While loving the fight for thee.
For some it's a trick while other's a treat,
Love is dressed as hate this Halloween.

It's always mutually exclusive,
Or was inclusion employed as a wield?
Did you know you're playing a game of chess?
With the chariot hosting a second queen.
Don't forget that the pawn you sacrificed,
Can also bring back the lost guillotine.

Aged Youth

Hammer this nail on the cross you chose,
Old isn't an excuse, a tool or a curse foretold.

There's something about everything that grows,
In time, cell, dust or rusted from its prime source.
Couldn't you tell by the way I look at every scar you
unfold,
Old tells a story I could drown myself in if the
storyteller so told.

There's something about the wisdom that stole,
A lisp from an insufferable know-it-all.
Couldn't you tell by the chuckle that left my gloom at
loss,
A smirk that only lasts around your wrinkled soul.

If I knew you better I would bring back the lost cause,
The worth of an aged youth in this modern harrow.

One for You

Strangers of the Twilight

He passed the test.
To become the man in my life regardless of our age.
It wasn't romantic but boy, was it encouraging,
To believe that love comes in all forms,
Especially this platonic relationship between two
generations residing in 60's,
Talking about character and marmalades or our destiny
in exchange.

I belong to the generation of cultured savages,
While my heart refuses to beat in the cyber or breathe
in the bottled space.
He belongs to the generation of men,
Refusing to bow to anything that feels comfortable
because discipline is his gospel,
A box to distract from living is not really his thing.

I was always old but my age became non-existent when
I learnt of him,
He spoke so charismatic and about the idiosyncratic
norms? Not a care.
I found a space for breeding my thoughts and feelings
like it wasn't yet in vain,
He could always sense a change in me,
That wasn't a haircut, a pimple but the change of flow
of blood in the artery but really; how did he?

What it means to live today is his jurisdiction against
dismay,
He is present in a way that his eyes could never give
away.
While he grew up in customary or the ordinary as they
would say,

Privilege is the idea that he knit of a modern man while
preserving the cavalier of other men he faced.

When I bring another into our sacred space,
He knocks in disapproval but his disappointment steals
the hay.
"You've got to stop rejecting every lad I bring", I
repelled,
"To reject or not, is a matter of a look in the eyes of
your own", he parlayed.
Because he too could read a man none the better than
anyone else today.

There's protection I feel without the cost of freedom in
his stay.
Every scar he parades, every touch he embraces,
Embodies the beauty of a man worth knowing today.
I learnt him when he told me he can't bet against a
certainty even in a harmless game,
That the principles in his life came from a twisted fate,
A string that tied me to him in this nameless
propinquity of two strangers,
Just hanging out in a bar on a Saturday.

Find yourself?

What does it mean?
Find yourself?
I have heard it my whole life,
And in the dozen books on my shelf.
Yet it consumes an erring amount,
Of time and mind to figure what could help,
Understand what it does mean,
When you've found yourself.

Crystal clear hope and,
A will that sustains,
A prospect that will land,
You into that magical plane,
But what if it isn't as grand,
As my hope force fed my will.
Did I find myself in the dune of sand?
Or am I still fueling the cloud of rain?

It will probably ease,
The restless nights and empty breathes,
To find yourself in evergreen peace,
Perennial as it come and letting you,
Make of it as you will while you continue to cease,
The reckless wondering,
Tattooed on your face with those temporal creases,
Hushing the loudness of the disturbed freeing genuine
feelings.

Find Yourself!

It's never easy to walk the path primping and cackling,
Pretending everything in your life is a host of indulging
memories,
It daunts on shallowing at the sight of that crippling
question,
When you truly don't have any moment worth
remembering especially amongst those festering.

But she primps and cackles,
She pretends everything hosts a majestic dream,
She isn't daunted when her shallow life is questioned
the dreaded,
Moment she experienced whether she laughed or just
wanted to scream.

By far, it's not what broke you that makes you stronger,
What breaks you only leaves a wound,
Its where you choose to go after you were hurt,
After all heaven can also be hell for people who forget
to live waiting for it to consume.

Where you learn to channel your incidents,
Wounds turn to tales you tell,
When you realize it's always the place that stumped
you,
If you just hadn't been there to begin with.

If you were unlucky to had been thrown,
Into its clutches just like she was,
Remember where you were sold and forgotten,
Go back, pick her up and walk away because,

You find yourself right in the moment that broke you,
You just hadn't left the scene at all.

<u>Promised to You.</u>

To be truly intimate with me,
Don't try to steal a physical touch,
Learn to touch my mind and soul,
That's the surest way to bring me down to my knee.

The more I loosen my tongue,
The more I secure your ground in my life,
Because words are those watchful birds I cage,
For the fear of being shot down before they could fly.

So, If I set them free in your space and view,
I have given you access to my barebones,
The trust you gained is far more intimate,
Than anything I can ever give you.

Let me see what I become,
When I learn more of yours and you,
And if the birds burn into a phoenix all of a sudden,
I am promised to you in the flight of the final descend.

<u>**_A Coffeehouse and a Bookstore_**</u>

A coffeehouse and a bookstore,
Every modern ballad's personifying edifice,
These two places house a myriad of stories,
A dreamer's dream come true; lest a realist's reality.

The easiest way to my heart and into my soul,
Take me to a coffeeshop followed by a bookstore,
Let's crash through the narratives of all those faceless,
While you look at mine and I at yours,
And every expression I bring to life,
While you infect me with your laugh as I watch you
bestow.

The aroma of the roasting bean adds its own element to
our rhyming scent,
A smell so unique that creates nostalgia even before we
left each other in that zone,
Every sip is whisking a savor of the sour,
But the moment sweetens it since it's our moment after
all,
We danced this chemistry into the bookstore,
As we scoot through rows and rows of books and dump
it in our destiny's haul,
Each story will ignite a lore between us, of our own,
Will you take me to a coffeehouse and follow it with a
bookstore?

The Lovers Meet

The evening announced itself with the lovers meet.
The girl in floral dress leapt and ran,
To hug the man in three pieces,
Fastening the clutch, with our eyes did we greet.

Let's stare down in each other's eyes,
Shifting and setting parallel to that sunset.
With your hazel to that orange in the sky,
Let it light my vision as we sunk into oblivion.

Just grab my waist and take the lead,
Like the moon is leading us into the night.
Let's warm our hearts in that crisp, cold wind,
And continue to gaze down deep into our souls as the
night turns white.

Be at ease and join me in this moment,
For I am in the present and in this moment, we'll always
be.
Run free and wild; Walk the calmest beach,
Exploring all heights, and laughing unconditionally.

We talked past nightfall, roamed the empty streets,
The world became non-existent with every word
released,
We can dance our way to the nearest coffeehouse we
see,
And add bagels and beans to this choreographed
chemistry.

The night will cease.
And so, will this freeze.
What will remain of us in the end,
Is the memory of you and me.

The Change

No one is coming,
In the state of discerning,
The ordeals that were governing,
My mind and the reality,
Harassing the peace just so politically,
Forging a calm chaos in this lenient tragedy.

No one should come,
Let the reality strike a war with the mind like a strum,
With a vibration so heavy that silences the hum,
To quiet the role of the ghost,
And realizing you have the power to vote,
The mind out of this controlling post.

No one came,
To lather the reality hoping to tame,
The frizz of the mind always ready to blame,
You and she and him and I and I once again.
But the steam opens the pore or was it the pain,
Wait, it's breaking the wall and cleaning the stain.

No one could come,
I didn't give them a chance,
No one could come,
So that I could become,
The change.

Will you Believe Me?

When I walk, I walk to find,
The parody of the event,
And the rhythm of the crime.
I match my steps,
And the pace of my whine,
To quickly empty the carts,
At the cashier of my divine.

The first cart was full,
The second sublime,
By the time I reached to third,
We ran out of time.
I fumbled and jumbled,
To get my holy to validate me sine,
An inch of humble acceptance,
A quarter? No less than a dime.

Waiting to be discounted,
To feel accounted in my prime,
I looked at the Mighty,
Signaling a minuscule smile.
He asked me how I wanted to pay,
In an answer or just an expression in mime?
I asked will you believe me?
When I couldn't credit any belief in myself,
Or this errand of mine?

His Eyes

His gaze drew me closer to him,
Without ever having looked into his eyes.
Smiled my conscious with words queueing at the rim,
Knowing I would never have to use them,
He stood tall while sulking, pretending he was wise.

Was its armored pride or shielded vulnerability, my
dear?
Keeps me up at night questioning was it right,
Having given you a part of my gig and the worst of my
fear,
With you showing your inability to cease what's been
so transparently laid,
Hoping I could keep my will a little more eager and a
little more bright.

The night ended and so did our time,
I couldn't speak while you couldn't decide,
Whether you should trust me and will our bodies
rhyme,
To the rhythm of that music that's stuck in our head
since we said hi,
Is it just this moment or will you want me every day by
your side?

Nonetheless what we made of our fate,
There's something that etched down my spine,
The sole comedian and the poet of this date,
Your eyes, they drew me closer,
Without ever meeting mine.

Tantrum

Slowly, the world is getting easier.
As blurry as it gets in my gaze,
The clearer I see as day,
And the vision that I needed to see today,
Was that of the child left behind,
Unattended, abandoned in the darkened hallway.

She was wrestling with the chains on the stairs.
A look at me and she forgot she was caged,
Weeping a cascading current from her sullen eyes,
She was washed but not drained,
Is what I learned from our first encounter,
And I knew everything I needed to amend for her stay.

But she threw tantrums whilst my patience was
wearing.
Everything was getting worse than earlier witnessed,
She grew tougher while the world was getting tougher
times two,
I needed to get her on board,
So that both of us could finally live a life,
That neither assumed would ever come true.

And then I blurred my vision further to arrest.
I arrested the world and the mystery unveiled,
She didn't want to witness the change,
She just wanted to feel what she couldn't feel,
In her own time and stay,
An experience is what makes the child move to another
stage.

And so my path became apparent in this maze.
I will dance for her so that she can laugh at herself,

I will paint my lips and nails red,
So that she can know color and its shades,
I will take her to see the world,
So that she can see herself in all those faces.

And most importantly I will love.
For in my love, she will set herself free,
In my embrace of another,
She will embrace every memory,
I will be her tantrum,
So that she can be legendary.

<u>*Quiet*</u>

Not everyone can hear you when you're quiet.

Listen when you stop hearing.
The silence can be deafening for those who listen.

Observe when you stop inferring.
The quacks are louder on the faces of those deceiving.

Drop a hint that you're believing.
The menaces are usually the gold in the coal you're
rejecting.

Watch out for the nomenclature,
The tags that derivate before the body's cold in the
morgue of the mirage encore.

When you're quiet, watch those who can hear your
labyrinth of noise off-sold.

Two Worlds Apart

She and I are two worlds apart,
Twisted in a tale of evermore where,
Gallivanting, been I whilst she followed her heart.
And all I can do is watch her from afar,
The whimsy and fire she uses as her dart.

She wants to blossom, she wants to bloom,
Could someone capture the state of her and,
Could you please zoom?
There's a song in her head she keeps dancing to,
Could you capture what's making her zap out of her
gloom.

If I have to guess that song, I'd bet its rock,
Beat after drop and louder than its soft,
Consuming and steering her from the hat to sock,
Can I join her rhythm without mocking her art?
Can I join her rhythm without a key to her lock?

Because I Know You

The intimacy in "How did you know that?" and
"Because I know you."
Is the easiest yet not the most accessible form of
expression around,
How beautiful is it to take time to learn someone's
language of existence?
To celebrate them in their own expression is the only
way to build a connection that's profound.

The presence you create in your simpleton,
That allows the most complex of people to seek out,
To be truly understood and not just heard,
In times of great war in our paradise.

The most beautiful gift of existence is memories,
Ensure to make it warm like a hug from a giant hugger
who is well endowed,
And the most important lesson of existence is caution,
Ensure to limit access to you to those whose love
language matches yours.

Because if you don't, you stand on other side of the see-
saw alone,
Approaching exhaustion craving for bare minimum
while fantasizing about beyond and above,
The inability to descry intimacy in every short moment,
That's how you starve or drain in love.

<u>The Evening was Ours</u>

Evenings have outlived one another,
With the same intense sunset,
That would dictate the night to fall over.
But this one time in the history of my hour,
I stole the routine to let someone in,
And watch me decide how I either,
Lose myself in the joy or be lost forever.

While escaping every face one after the other,
I danced myself across the fancies and follies,
The wind had exhausted the calm it had,
To get colder, meaner yet a lot less nervous,
And as I strolled my abode to the fanciest corner,
You snatched my attention with nothing but a cleaner
manner.

For the first time in the longest minute,
I greeted calmness in the setting hour,
All it needed was a gent to be gentle,
In how he treated the lady against her sour,
Disdain ideal of a life she assumed to exist,
And hoped that it will one day, devour her.

The evening was mine for he paved it for me,
For my nerves and every affliction,
And watched me unfold a woman,
I hid behind a distorted version for survival,
That evening he introduced me to I,
Who existed in his gaze that could pierce,
Through my insecurities and my silence.

Full Moon's Night

She noticed a pattern,
In that pattern she projects,
Her cry for help from something that doesn't exist.
She functions from emotions,
While absolutely unaware,
Of how to control them or the need to resist.
The chaos inside is burning,
So loud and blue,
Only to settle down and eventually extinguish.

And now she waits,
And as she waits she paints,
Every color that the flame ignites.
She waits to stop escaping the truth,
So that she can finally escape,
The comfort in which she resides.
It's natural to be curious,
Frustrated and confused at her sight,
There will be a new dawn for her under the full moon's
nightlight.

She grows distant,
When she learns her place,
In your eyes.
She stays quiet,
When you ridicule,
The unfiltered state of hers.
She frustrates those,
Who watch her surrender so easily to some,
But build a wall for others up high.

Yet she loves so gently,
That you forget to dream,
She whispers a new story from her mind's library.

She follows and leads,
To absorb and allow,
For you to truly live with her so vividly.
She smiles from ear to ear,
Even if you don't give her a reason,
She makes it up and in that she owns a mastery.

<u>*Tough Love*</u>

She wasn't the toughest to love,
She required a love that was tough,
A grip that was gentle,
Yet a hold that you would never let go of.

In her silence, she speaks,
And in yours, she shatters,
The day she whispers what she feels,
She found her voice in you away from her whisper less
chatters.

While the world around consumes her,
She looks for you when the night gets colder,
Because a home is not a house but those warm arms,
To restore her as she runs out easily on giggles and
laughter.

If she still feels challenging in one way or another,
Remember she requires patience for her world crumbles
often,
The toughest to love only need you to hold them,
And let them heal on the cushion of your beating heart
in silence

Trapped

 You looked like a distant hope.
I wanted you because you looked like the pieces,
That would fit the crevices in my hope.
You looked like the channel wide enough,
To let my ship sail right across that terrifying shore.

I wanted you because I found myself trapped,
Between my existence in the lightyear past us,
And the fathomable impact of the time continuum
explored.

I wanted you because you were supposed to fix.
Every crack in my walls, each muscle memory hiding
my face from all those.
Your presence was supposed to fix the jeopardy I
outshone.

Left am I in this choir of clowns,
Singing the blues of a fairytale gone wrong.
You participated in the misery and added to cement on
my forlorn,
A tale of a woman wanting him for fucks sake, at least I
hope.

Can We Love the Same?

Plato

Soulmates!
A concept that may be delusional.
Concept?
More of a feeling that's unusual.

When no man could put together
Words to inch closer to an explanation,
Plato hid his confusion and
Sought his famous symposium for revelation.
He wrote " Humans were born with four
Legs and hands and two faces.
The combined strength bore
the capacity to conquer the subsequent races.

Fearing the ability,
Zeus felt threatened.
Split in two,
Two parts he reckoned.
Condemned them to find the other half,
For the rest of their lives.
He thought he did his part,
That will save his pride."

Little did he know
What we are made of.
You tell us not to do it,
We sought it above all.

Lucky are those who in spite find the missing piece,
Which frightened the might.
Look carefully it can be around resting impatiently,
Waiting to be found.

What a feeling it must be to have defeated the Lord,

To be forgiven instantly,
As you connect back your chord.

<u>*A Venture of Mine*</u>

An ever so confusing thought that arises,
Why did we confine love in a world that's uprising?
And what if I defy to behold the torch that torments
them all,
What if I love not just one but each that makes my heart
feel at home in a world that's lost?

Could I create a world where love has no jurisdiction
for jeopardy?
Where each has a place of their own, dwelling in
intimacy,
But that intimacy is not a synonym for swive,
Just a connection so profound that sends the shiver
between you and I.

How about a venture in disguise?
I would admit to anyone who doesn't limit my chime,
In exchange, I would offer a space that feels like home,
So that you work in the comforts of an arm like mine.

The humdrums of these unparalleled crimes,
Would unleash the greatest evil alike,
Or would I ultimately find,
Just the crowd that is less blind?

<u>*Love*</u>

It's wondrous how
I know so little about love,
Yet I behold the prowess of
Differentiating the right from unknown.
Is it in my nature to know love?
And if it is,
Is it identical
To the wings whose valiance
Flutters through turbulence, still
Swearing its allegiance to fly high and over the hill.

Is it identical
To the armor against the sword
That keeps the knight
Eager, protected and obliged
To his oath
To his love
And to his might.

Or is it disparate
To hate?
Reflecting the fire of aggressive passion
To jealousy?
Suggesting the hint of unsettlement
To betrayal?
Establishing the end of the session.

It's foul to humanly decide
That it's all there is to love.
For you to reckon it's worth,
You must first embrace every curve.

It does indeed rest in nature itself.
Love is built-in.

Foundation of our being,
Rooted in each muscle,
Engraved in each bone.

It is identical to identity,
Meaning to mean;
And to stay
Around to belong.

A Poet's Serendipity

The parlor of the intrigued,
Held a debate over the fateful nature,
Could a poet ever be in disdain,
Over the yearning of another.

Will he perish the world?
Or will the world perish for him,
When he longs for his lover?
Oh, but how could he know love,
When he hasn't known hunger?

One such romantic argued, 'Must you always be hurt,
To truly birth a wonder?
Love is light, love is more,
And the sooner we learn this right,
The lesser one suffers through forlorn.'

To which another parlayed,
'How would you know love is light and more,
If there never existed dark and almost?
Every poet is paradoxically inclined,
Because for endings to exist there must be,
A beginning and a pioneering pain,
For anyone to greet an ending that is happier than vain.'

The parlor had silent spectators,
With lovers who couldn't issue any advice,
The others felt too lip sealed to propel any inquisition,
They assumed he had a right to remain silent,
For his love couldn't blossom no matter the luck,
He smiled over the silenced audience and said,
'Yes, there used to be love but do you know what
comes after?"

Silence grew louder and fell upon the room,
The bearers of serendipity knew of only love and luck,
The world always knew that there exists a soul for
every other,
Fates were woven in heaven and bestowed upon the
one's stationed on Earth,
Which ultimately is the only ask we put in our gospels,
So why would someone in their sane mind ask for
anything after?
The silent spectator broke his calm countenance and
answered,

'Love is only the beginning to find salvation thereafter.'

<u>*Lover's Love*</u>

I always wondered,
Why people who are loved,
Have a different wind,
Blowing in their hair.

The eyes that twinkle,
Not for someone but with that one,
To blur the sky that exists,
For tomorrow.

The laugh like rhythm,
In perfect harmony,
With the happiness like treble,
To compose a wholesome music.

For just between those two.

But have you ever noticed,
The ones who love?
The song may not be about them,
But it wouldn't exist without these seers.

Such wondrous zealots,
Willing to go unnoticed to notice,
The one they love,
Just to be the reason behind that passionate zest.

The ones who are loved,
May be the masterpiece.
But it's the ones who love,
That are the sculptors,

Of this heavenly view.

<u>*Love Heals*</u>

Love heals,
Or so I am told,
Why is it hard to believe?
Is it possible to ease the pain with just your hold?
I will know.

Someday, I will look back on this day,
The hollow July,10 days into the play,
From hiding the clouds of my ache,
To seeking the sun before it's all decayed.
I will know.

Understand why it all played out the way it did,
Maybe it was to teach me to be more caring and gentler,
Or plausibly to find my ever after,
Happily, or disarrayed,
I will know.

You are supposed to heal the cracks in my being,
I don't know how and I'm not supposed to ask,
But all I want is for you to make me laugh while
ensuring,
You love me so every night that is befalling and,
I will know.

I have been left on an edge more times than I can count,
Don't leave me hanging while I wait for you now and
evermore,
Let's disappear for hours doing our own thing,
While reserving the night for each other, exchanging
stories woven in our prime and,
I will know.

I will heal my own cracks and find my own purpose,

I just need you to be with me while I am struggling to
keep up,
And while trying to support, don't buy me all kinds of
pretty stuff,
Just give me your hoodie that smells like you and,
I will know.

A Fiery Touch

I could feel his touch while he wasn't even in the room,
A mist of passion sprinkled slightly all over the palace
of swoon.
The bell ran an electric wave from the spine till above
the neck so my hair moved,
This evening I had no intention of dressing the part of
my heart that yearns for you.

You stood on the other side of the door,
So, I lingered to see if your breath can pierce through,
Instead I lathered in the scent of the man who smells
indeed like,
A hint of chivalry, a pint of control and a gallon of
cavalier is all over you.

Could you light up this room any more than you already
do?
 I felt so vulnerable yet so safe in this lantern of youth,
You held in your palms as you walked across the floor,
To find your center in my arms that was tainted all blue.

But that one touch ran the colors across the vessels and
so,
I became more aware of the breath in my view.
Mixing the breathing with alternating thoughts and
glances,
That one look told me I was going to lose myself in all
these advances.

I leaned slowly and slower to reach you in your time,
Because you keep a distance and I don't want to stand
beyond that line.
Every soft look in your eyes gave me an inch closer to
you,

I got past the point where it's now just you and me and
nothing between us two.

I kissed your cheeks to adore your entirety,
To pull back to still respect your privacy.
But your gaze demanded more of my love and for me to
keep you covered,
So, I placed another peck and stood still to let the
calmness hover.

I noticed a flinch in the nerves of your face,
Like you wanted to back out without moving out of this
pace,
So, I started to pull away because your comfort meant
more,
Than this alchemy that could anytime turn sore.

You threw a sigh like you're ready to give in,
Because control doesn't last long against love,
So, you pulled me by my waist and leaned,
To engrave a kiss that would finally let the heart
intervene.

<u>Speak to Me in Poetry</u>

I exist outside of these pages,
That I fill now with the remains of every memory I celebrated,

While carving my love in scribbles instead of sketches,
The depth of that love will be found in that full stop etched,
In those very last pages.

You exist inside of these pages,
Filling the void in my life awaiting that one day,
I don't have to hold a pen to feel your presence,

Or smell an old parchment sheet every day,
Yet you come alive only when the ink runs in these blank spaces.

Someday, someone will find all that I scripted,
I hope it's you who finds this mirror I bled through to put together,

And as you scroll I hope you find me instead,
Speak to me through poetry,
Because at one point, we have both lived there.

<u>*The Vibrant Act*</u>

A paradigmatic of today's world,
Love filtrated by obsession,
Turning slowly into possession,
And is everything but unique,
For today's love is simply oblique,
So as to speak.

First, they find themselves attracted,
And attraction stems from a lack,
A lack of sense of self so as to distract,
You find charm in someone,
Who has something you wish to have,
And that begins the story of being trapped.

That attraction turns into obsession,
Because what you lack is what you attract,
Creating a void whenever the other fails to adapt,
The world terms it loves,
For it creates the illusion of a vibrant act,
And makes you crave, need, and want the contact.

But there's a fine line one must understand,
Love is peace, and a splurge rarely adds,
If you find something attractive that may create a void,
There's already a void you must understand,
Feeling the content in yourself is how it begins and
that's a fact,
You cannot love with attraction we must understand.

Souls Don't Meet by Accident

There's something my mum said,
It's the same something that keeps popping up in my
head,
Time and again, no matter how stupid it felt,
Souls don't meet by accident she yelled.

What if it's true?
The romantic in me whispered with my sense waiting in
a ditched queue,
Did I meet you already or am I still grazing to find you?
Its ecstatic to think if I walked past you while I wasn't
even in your view.

While every other soul has been a temporary chapter,
Shorter than I expected and then it went even shorter
after,
These pages have stories but I didn't write them in
glitter,
Because I couldn't find that sparkle in any of those
character.

She could be right if truth be told,
I haven't met anyone who didn't teach me how to
unfold,
Every blind eye I was willing to dispose,
To each who abused my care while trying hard to hold.

To me, it's irrelevant if I have found you already,
I am walking towards you and I will only reach when
I'm ready,
Halting in between to eat, watch that sunrise or
collecting royalty,
Creating a mix tape just to end up singing all that's
written by Kiki Dee.

When it's time just say this to me,
'Souls don't meet by accident' and watch how I turn to glee,
And to know if I truly believe,
Just check if I wrote your name in glitter in my diary.

An Ode

Yes, being loved by someone who describes you,
As the link between heaven and Earth,
Is the mist in fog that just captivates you,
And entrances you into believing the unbelievable.

But it is the people who love that creates the link,
To connect you to the gates of heaven,
Without them, Earth and heaven can never meet,
For the builders are oblivious of their powers indeed.

A small ode to the odysseys of these phenomenal
creators,
That stand next to god in creation of something others
can't understand,
Without them, you are whole and complete,
With them, you know wholeness even after you divide
from within.

<u>Construct of Love</u>

He understood,
And that's what sealed them,
In the pages that were waiting,
Patiently for someone,
To put a name to the running ink,
That would match her rhythm.

He believed,
That she wouldn't believe,
In any construct of love,
That is anything but free,
And became the first person,
To love her without imprisoning.

He managed,
To match the degree,
Of her unconditional love,
To not confine anyone or,
Limit the love to just courtship,
He knew how to love without jurisdiction.

They became,
The first people of their kind,
To achieve freedom in love,
Amidst those arresting each other,
In an attempt to license,
This emotional, mental, and physical intimacy.

The Slow, Old Love

I want that slow love.
The kind that takes its time to acquaint itself with the
hosts.
I want to feel safe than sparked in that momentary buzz,
Every stolen glance of grace and a touch to bring you
back in every moment you outgrow.

I want that old love.
Where we didn't choose each other rather woven in
luck.
There's no swiping left or right or gaslighting with
intoxicating words,
Just the little things we do for each other in the moment
before us.

I would assume the roles we were taught how to chuck,
In the name of equality, we forgot how to build a house
into home in this renovated world.
Would you bring the unbranded silhouette of the 60's in
our paddock?
And loosen the tightened jar on the shelf up above.

I would assume every chance to make it work,
There're quitters too many so would you stand out of
this herd?
Two can also be a crowd if you haven't chosen the right
one,
So, find the fit because decorated decades are a sight
that shouldn't be blurred.

Chemistry

Forfeit yourself to the idea that,
Chemistry belongs between any two,
Who can concoct this draft.

Not just a contractual bond,
But all the others that offer a thread,
In an attempt to spark a nerve,
And light it in the brightest shade of red.

Chemistry isn't only romance,
But that banter you strike,
  In the comfort of another.
The barter you hike,
Just to smirk at the falter of other.
Or simply to be lulled,
In the moment between 2 minds and hearts,
But a single thought of being together.

Intimacy is maligned,
By those who don't truly love.
It is a bystander of all that is aligned,
With the purest power of affection.
Engraved in all those inclined,
With intention to connect rather,
Besmirch this wonder.

Freedom to Love

The lurking sight for the sorest eye,
Is sometimes just an attempt in disguise?
To see freedom in the constructs of the world,
And what more freer than the freedom to love?

Watching the bickering husbands of distressing wives,
And the patiently waiting for their turns to come alive,
How sick were we in our really early lives?
To cage love so as to love one person offering your
throat to a slow slitting knife?

The wisest of the breathing and the fearsome alike,
Are falling overhead in suffocation and unnatural
might,
The only thing you had to do was simply love them
right,
Not one person but all who shared the level of your
heart's joy.

The only construct that is destroying our lives,
Is the one we created for love in order to deprive,
Others a chance to have what you think belongs to you
and I,
The love you share is not real, did you not realize?

<u>*Is Love worth Living or Dying for?*</u>

So, he said he'd die for you?
And in his death, you see your honor?
But shouldn't you see his love for you?
A man who wants to live every day to face each
inconvenience of the manor.

To die is too easy when you're intoxicated on the
secretes,
A really low blow on love to be left behind by an
abuser of this drug.
To love is to live for each fortnight and the promise to
ease,
The damsel that is life when it whines or shrugs.

They often confuse obsession as a martyr of this
beloved,
He heightened and tightened his grip or his clutches,
Because he really couldn't love,
And fathom the radical discipline in sunrise and
sunsets.

Love is paradoxical in nature,
But does not invite insobriety in dullness,
If calm is not noticeable in the halts of this adventure,
You're not in love but just obsessed on the chunks of
pleasure you harness.

If you ever wonder what truly kills you on the way to
paradise,
Death takes a second or a minute for some,
It's living that truly takes your entire life,
Dying is an excuse for those who want an easy way out
of this humdrum.

<u>Control</u>

Once the ancient one offered a time,
For two people to fall in love,
He initiated the journey with a whisk of a thyme,
Waiting for one to finally set another free.

Days passed by,
The two couldn't make it work,
One fell too hard,
And the other repelled for the fear that lurked.

The day finally arrived,
When the ancient one asked the couple of their love,
The other who was repelled,
Commenced her vocal battle.

"I was trying so much to love,
But I couldn't decide whether to choose freedom,
Or his unconditionally yet all-consuming love,
I tried but my seize was never an option."
"I too tried to love less,
But I couldn't decide whether to choose restriction of
my affection,
Or the moment before me and her,
And so, I chose to control my path irrespective of her
objection."

The ancient one broke the silence,
"When you try to control a situation,
And the situation embraces another person,
Controlling makes the other strangulated,
Thus, causing the distance.
When you find yourself in a situation with another,
Let go,

Let the process unfold organically,
For it will not arrest, it will set you both free of
resistance. "

And that's love.

One for Me

In a Sharply Weird Time

Oakwood scented candles in a place she called her own,
A stairway ringed with wooden banister as she skipped
her chuckle down to the room.
She lined the frames of faces she loved and set the fire
to the hearth that was cold,
She began to moist the tip of the flowers that smell like
a summer valley tickling the womb.

There was something about architecture she learned to
adore as she grew,
Every blueprint, every wall has a story brewing a house
in view.
She remembered the days she watched the men
assemble her majestic lay,
Piece by piece the wrap-around porch, the intricate
woodwork and the rooftop tower she drew.

The towners would define her as a lady of the manor,
Ever so mysterious but kind as a new born laughing at
the dew.
Her body would talk before her lips made the move,
The dresses would dance with the wind and her walk in
a harmony that would let you assume her next groove.

She danced her evenings into the cool nights,
Laughing and bickering with hers truly, both
reminiscing in their prime.
In a world where love is requited and easily renounced,
She knew love to be freeing and twinning of hearts as
they rhyme.

As spring advances, she begins to excite,
To travel the world and see it in all her favorites colors
of red, black and white.

She struts her way in the foreign lands hoping to find,
A meaning to add to her dictionary as she defines life.

For a woman with words, she taught herself early in her
life,
To survive well and to stand, never fear the tender
power of lone and the might.
While dancing and singing and finding a partner to
suffice,
She knew the weightage of educating oneself in the
matters of the world in sight.

Even though she is a woman of the modern day and
night,
You can always find her with scrunchies, red lip,
vintage bell bottom and some jewelry all gold,
With a load of classic tales and work of art in her sack
that's never light,
For she is a modern woman living with a soul that's old,
In a sharply weird time.

The Night Sky

As a child, I loved the night sky more than daylight,
For in the night, the reality is blurry,
And you see what you want to see in those corrupted
sight.
I waited each morning for the dawn to break,
So that dusk could rise like a phoenix rising after
burning,
And I could witness the new phoenix out of the ashes
wide awake.

I would wait so eagerly to wander and meet the dark,
In the hope to find something and anything,
In all the possible worlds apart.
At first it was exciting to ride into the ceaseless,
There were stars, and dust, and an opportunity of
another world,
Where I could just simply be, abandoning the inner
analyst to the hearth.

I wandered and wandered and wandered too far,
Only to meet the real darkness that no one prepared me
for,
There's no starlight once you've arrived on the side of
the paradox.
It's like a new, dark world and I have no idea how to
be,
Whether to breathe to live or eat or sleep,
How does it function or what does this side breed?

The total darkness is a potential decree,
A torture worse than oblivion for it paralyses,
While not restricting, you're absolutely free,
And lets you guard every small memory,
Which slowly turns into the best torture,

A punishment greater than capital for life's worst
treachery.

How do you come back from a place?
For which you do not have survival instincts?
Just floating around in this endless space.
If I could invade this world in the hope to find,
Could something else also invade in the hope to find
me?
To bring me light and greet darkness only when I'm
truly ready?

I was Planted

It was dark and cold,
No reflection of the soul,
Just regret and seeping delusion,
Fading my sight and blinding my vision.

There was a weight I felt over my chest,
Then my hands and feet and head that were at rest,
Smelling like clay and soil, was it my hard work?
Turns out I was just buried where no one would lurk.

I panicked when I realized where I was,
Did I win this life or was it a loss?
But I was too young to have crossed my path,
With a reaper of those who stopped counting their
breath.

I cried and cried and tried to get back,
While death was certain, I wasn't done yet,
Yes, it was hard and I assumed to have ended,
This misery and pain while trying to hold onto a
happier ending.

Whilst I lay there in the ground,
Slowly ceasing to exist in the memories of those
around,
I wished for another chance at life,
Because I knew I wasn't done taking my biggest dive.

Moments had passed fading my sadness away,
I came to terms while appreciating the bouquet,
I started feeling the gravity and all its faucet,
I knew it was time for me to cross the final doorway.

And just like people claimed in more than one syllable,

There's a light at the end of every tunnel,
I was inching closer to find He who prevailed,
And ask all the questions whose answers were just
delayed.

The weight on my body was shedding so slow,
It felt like ether but I wished I could order that one last
coffee while I was on the go,
Maybe I wasn't ready yet to depart,
Or to find the answers I had been seeking because it
just wasn't the right ask.

With so much light reflected,
It took me by surprise when part of it refracted,
By the water that rained down the earth,
Was I given a second chance to explore my worth?

As I began to float further from the ground,
I watched a child hosing around,
With the sun in my eyes and the energy forming its own
wit,
I realized I wasn't buried, I was planted.

Sleepless Nights

When these sleepless nights kick in, she waits,
To move, to breathe, to not fear,
And most importantly, she waits
To be able to close her eyes again.
For her shivering hands and feet,
To feel a warmer hand,
A touch just so she could simply sleep.

When these sleepless nights kick in, it freezes,
While everything seems hushed,
Something manages to mangle at ease,
Toying with her feelings,
Tearing what was left,
From the previous day of,
Yet another arrest.

When these sleepless nights are over, it stays,
Feeding on the day while reserving the night,
To start over again but in tweaked new ways,
She smiles through it knowing someday,
Nothing's going to crawl under her skin or the bed,
Everything's going to be warmer,
Her feelings, his touch and all that's written but not
read.

<u>Aftermath of Tragedy</u>

As difficult as it may be to survive a tragedy,
There's something even more difficult in the aftermath
of this event,
As hard as it may be for the survivor to feel happy,
How do you understand her and love her when you
haven't felt the same sickness or what it meant?

She builds a wall of personality to hide everything else
within,
She's got friends and a loving family,
Yet she is the hardest to love to even begin,
Because her wall is too high to climb and no one cared
to go against and defy gravity.

She never asks or tells how she would want to be loved,
Her list of what she deserves is blank; for a burden, she
would never become,
So how does anyone climb this wall without her feeling
deceived?
Build a ladder of observation and notice her at every
turn.

Survivors of trauma naturally excel in the state of
anxiety,
For them, reassurance is resonant to a warm blanket on
a cold night,
She too needs it in bulk but not given in charity,
Anxiety is the painful nervous system wound that is
now her primary state until midnight.

Can you imagine living in survival for as long as the
day breaks into night sky,
He is frustrated when she doesn't express her truth for it
to be known,

The deafening silence she creates is the answer to all
the why's,
She would rather keep quiet than have her attacked for
just expressing how she feels or for any feeling that is
shown.

It's crazy to tell that she wants to be invisible but seen,
Left alone but heard, and held when she resists,
Because all she wants is all she believes,
That she doesn't deserve for she hasn't paid the price so
she insists.

Tie all the rungs of the ladder of stability,
Climb one step at a time and let her know even while
she's quiet,
Let her feel she can trust you in this world of
anonymity,
I promise she will bring a vibrant world just for you
two and somehow keep it private.

3 Funerals

I never realized that I died.
Once then a second and then a third time,
Oh, I am alright, just a little lopsided,
In my fourth life.

I died once when I stopped breathing as a child,
The day I gasped not my wiggly toe,
Or at the peeper at my bed side,
I gasped when I walked out of the line,
That was guarding my first life.

But I didn't know that was the last day,
When I was protected as a cub of the pride.

Second, I died when I couldn't find,
Any joy in the toy disguised in this world of mine,
I walked as a young woman in a perfect file,
Disciplined to live in a world of mimes.

But I didn't know that was the last day,
When I would ever enjoy the world outside.

The last I died when I forfeited my prime.
Young turned old enough to be the perfect bride.
With gravel in my chest, I looked at all the precise
signs.

But I didn't know that was the last day,
That I again didn't tell her goodbye.

When they had all died.

And now when I act like a child,
They ask me why, why can't I just comply,

Time is scarce while I shiver inside,
I have 3 funerals awaiting,
Each hoping I would let her go like I would my ally.

Friendly Demons

She was found a wounded mouse amongst armed rats,
With limping heart and severed hopes,
She snoozed in coma knowing it right,
It was time to bury the dead and the past,
Because she knew she lost it all this time.

Her body was lying in the pits,
Of anxiety and fear and the unknown,
That swallowed her within,
She was declared dead later that second,
Her body was set on fire till only her ashes remained.

The pit was surrounded by strangers and some strange
people akin,
Some choking, some screaming and rest gasping in
contempt,
They watched her rise from her ashes committing the
unforsaken sin,
She was devil's advocate for having risen not escaped,
The hell that consumed her like she conquered the
underworld's fiend.

She paraded her scars from the battle as she marched
ahead,
Her gaze had warmth that could torch the tortures of
your day,
The warmth got warmer until it burnt every spectator
dead,
She devoured the fire they set to the pit,
And now she uses the heat to ignite, spite or simply
behead.

No one could understand the creature that walked away,
For her soul was healed in hell while her heart was

stitched,
And her limbs sewn back in pain that could not be
conveyed,
She befriended her demons and they all walked
together,
To remind her that comeback is always stronger than
setback no matter how late.

The Night

"This is what I was missing!"
Laid in her bed, her arms suddenly let loose,
Hung by the sides, as the first drop of tear finally left her lash,
Creasing the temple, the drop ran as if it knew it was born to run that far that fast.

The more she stared, the bigger the void became.
She realized that it wasn't the void that was deepening.
Instead seeping her unrest soul to rest,
It was her aching heart that was healing.

The sirens of the chaos, the flashlight of the uncertainty,
Nothing flinched, not for a while.
Her bottom lip unlocked, and began to widen,
To smile at her destiny as she invites it back from exile.

The fingers moved, as if it had life of its own,
Her wrist in front of her face, wiping the life she had known.
How could you move when you have finally met with calm?
Her chest swiftly lifted her up reminding the world was already resting in her palm.

As she lifted her chest, her hair dragged behind hugging her neck,
The world seemed tingly as it should have been, in its best.
She looked around her crowded apartment with empty eyes,
She knew she found her wealth in love, health, dignity and wise.

The silhouette of her shoulder and waist,
Became more real as she draped her dress tighter,
Letting it go as she breathed the breath she'd been
gasping to take,
She cried "I did it", her future oozing brighter.

<u>Before Dawn</u>

Light is born at the wake of dawn,
Wrapping the darkness with a conceding frown,
Enveloping the surface of all those living around,
And often replaced as a euphemism in the expression of
the love that surrounds.

People love for love brings light,
But if you ask for my two cent or my daring insight,
People fall in love with the darkness inside,
Loving the light is easy for the warmth it derives,
When you truly fall in love with someone in your
limelight,
It's the darkness before dawn you recognize that you
learn to love in the hindsight.

That's how you fall in love, little did we know,
You understand, perceive, and embrace the murk they
show,
But who do you love through this high and low?
Simply, the one whose shades of darkness matches
yours,
And how far are they willing to go.

<u>Some of You</u>

Some of you hurt me for the first time.
Taught me how a heart aches and how brittle is it to
break.
The first time you chose another and then other.
Minute by second, I watched you choose someone else
over me.

Some of you held me when I had no faith to be held by
one.
Put me on a pedestal and let me believe that I was
wrong,
To have assumed that I couldn't have what the rest of
you so easily pursued.
Only to realize that the pedestal was in fact gallows all
along.

Some of you quit on me too early,
For you could have been part of my life where I could
have loved you harder,
Understood you better and stuck by you longer.
But you left and I forgot how to love harder, understand
better and stick longer.

Some of you expected too much.
Expected me to understand without you speaking,
Learn your emotions without having it expressed and,
Be gentle when your soul demanded.
I try so hard but I fail to understand what's not spoken
and none of you asked why.

Some of you left me too tired.
To try and go back to where it was none of you.

His Being is Enough

Warm was his embrace in my dull, dreary tide,
He gasps at my witty tickler,
And jogs a giggle at the corner of his smile.
The wick on his face lights at my twitching nose and
eyes,
Finding solace in the tall wax of his feelings,
Entertaining the flickers as my comfort in disguise.

The eyes are my favorite like a glazing starlight,
I can see the depth of his love in one look,
And the prevalence of my entirety in that sight.
His glance touches my skin before his fingers run by,
Softening the distorts of my aging, fine lines,
Turning the air more warm than when we started the
night.

The silence is worth every sunset I could sacrifice,
Golden hour for me is his arms covering my bare body,
Thawing the chills on my spine.
Every word then built forms a foreign paradigm,
Because language is what we craft,
With our bodies in synchronized mime.

Mystic in realm but oh! so human in simpler times,
His being is enough for me to protect,
Myself in my imagined reality or the one already in
design.
The nerves in his arm shoot a signal right to mine,
Easing me in believing he is right there,
Should I lose myself in the crowd of other's entwined.

A Niche of Characters

Gushing over time,
In an effort to align,
My thoughts and actions,
In the pervading space
Of this timeline.

Am I benign?
Because I fetch myself,
As a subject of your
Banter and quiet
My whispering mind.

A niche of characters,
Is the forte I design,
To arrest my attention
And fire my sensational
Soul to submit to my divine.

A quiet that I am,
With a fortress of words,
Intertwined while I define,
Who has access to this
Limitless projection of the universe inside.

I conjure a world within
Out of which I keep the world outside,
A virgin that world must remain,
To watch what pureness can
Birth into this Palestine.

The mystery I swore,
In the kingdom I mined,
The innocent love that I bore,
So that I can breathe you back to life,

And let you be immortal in mine.

Her Secret

A poet's nature,
Is nurtured in oblivion.
In nothing, she finds,
Paradox that instills,
Her vision.

She then uses,
This vision of irony,
To ignite a conversation,
With anyone willing,
To sink in her eyes amongst many.

The one who lost,
Gained a plethora.
Especially a part of,
The heart that has,
Voyaged every era.

She chose him,
If you ask for my two cents.
For in oblivion, you find,
The divine and the divine,
In your time is the one true gent.

Once she chose,
And he folds,
Expect to be her art.
To live forever in the pages,
She wrote.

She will cease,
As a poet
When the time comes.
But you, you will remain,

As her art, her secret,

For the world to uncover.

<u>*She is a Lady*</u>

She is a lady.
A lady of tall stature,
Burnt in her prime building towering walls,
With an unlikely window of curvature.

Through that curve, she molds her mind,
Who gets in and who stays out.
If you look at her, her narrative is facetiously printed like a
crime.
There's only one of him that fits her golden hour stout.

She is a lady.
A lady who's always armed around.
She books her words for the uncommonly loud,
While protecting herself against who she surrounds.

Yet if you notice her turnabout,
He paints a world for her where it's only them,
And a couple of verbs framing the gallery in the town.
Her guards come down while she starts to blossom from
her stem.

She is a lady.
One for the world.
She fights, she acts, she smirks, and she claps,
While switching her outfits of charm and bold.

She is a lady.
One for him.
Her heart smiles, the head giggles, and her stomach flies,
While nothing is about her anymore but just the soul in
rhyme.

Space for Me?

The first time you met me,
I was a handful for your little world,
A world that was already full with people who were
undeserved,
To know you or your husky laughter,
And then you began questioning whether you can carve
a space,
To even try to fit the misfit that I was in your little
place.

And so, you dared for the very first time,
The world you lived in became real despite,
Every power around you to keep you in their palms real
tight,
You dared for once to act more than you think,
Of the consequences of the greet between you and I,
It dawned on you that you could be happier than your
lives made up lies.

But when it got real,
You had to make a choice,
And you chose to feel nothing and hush your heart's
noise,
If you felt nothing why did you shake?
Why did your breath break its rhythm at the clack of
my heels?
And why only you know my scent when there was no
embrace in our deals.

There is a banter that can never be shared,
When you smile in response to my smile,
Like a secret between us in that comfort in disguise,
You knew you found what everyone is searching for,
A home without an address and a reason without

implies,
But would you own this place or rent it like you did
your life?

<u>Will You Believe Me?</u>

When I walk, I walk to find,
The parody of the event,
And the rhythm of the crime.
I match my steps,
And the pace of my whine,
To quickly empty the carts,
At the cashier of my divine.

The first cart was full,
The second sublime,
By the time I reached to third,
We ran out of time.
I fumbled and jumbled,
To get my holy to validate me sine,
An inch of humble acceptance,
A quarter? No less than a dime.

Waiting to be discounted,
To feel accounted in my prime,
I looked at the mighty,
Signaling a minuscule smile.
He asked me how I wanted to pay,
In an answer or just an expression in mime?
I asked will you believe me?
When I couldn't credit any belief in myself,
Or this errand of mine?

<u>***My Safe Space***</u>

You gave me a safe space.

A place of warmth,
More for my rejected thoughts,
Than for my freezing skin.
A home to return,
When I absolutely couldn't,
And wouldn't ask another to take me when I was on the
broken rim.

You gave me a safe space.

To talk about that lingers,
In my mind and heart,
And in all the 24 worlds inside.
To teach me as though,
You have read my thoughts,
To be this gentle to a gentile.

You gave me a safe space.

So that I can maximize,
Every sound I hushed,
In the everyday life.
Letting me crack the hour,
While you laughed until the sunset,
Oh, I couldn't forget the hype.

In all that you do,
And in all that you live,

You became my safe space.

The Captive Me

She is there,
I locked her in a cage,
And threw away the key in despair.
I wasn't ready to find out just yet,
All the potential and possibility she bears.

I think she can hear,
Every cry and need that I openly dismiss,
Muttering the words, very patiently she stares,
At the wounds I carved on my canvas,
She hones my attention with a warning like glare.

I can feel her shifting in the chair,
The captive is turning into the captor,
She saw the circus I was running out here,
So now she is bargaining her release,
Telling me she can get us both somewhere.

I realized I need to let her take her share,
This phase is hers, a 12-year-old shouldn't drive,
I figured why I have been driving so much into dead
ends.
So, I sat in the backseat while she took the wheel,
I'm going to watch what she births and how much will
she actually dare.

<u>***An Outlaw***</u>

The farther I reach,
The further I want to go.
Every point I breach,
In the limits I set on my own.
Mildly amused at the events,
That keeps me on my toes.
Calibrating my fate and turning it,
Into a blueprint from a new get go.

Wildly assumed that I was enough all alone,
Only to surrender to your whims long ago.
Cruel was the world,
To keep you from my hold,
It was funny to watch me try,
Until you took control.
The boat I was trying to sail,
Was actually supposed to be rowed.

The furthest I am,
The farthest I feel in my growth,
The ultimate price I paid was,
The boundary I made them follow.
It emptied my nest,
But it was never left hollowed.
You knew how to build so you built,
A throne in my nest that turned into our little cosmos.

It was never supposed to begin,
To end up in the shadows,
I was never meant for a goal,
Or the destination more so,
I was always supposed to become,
An observer, a lover, and the poet,
And more importantly, an outlaw.

To This I Submit

'Doesn't it scare you?
Trusting people?
I see you sharing your heart wide and open,
I wish I could be secure while being real,
Don't you worry that someone might walk away leaving
you feeling like an orphan.'

Weaving one blanket of anxiety after another,
Each railing to have something to hold on to,
She looked at me smiling like a flower that would
wither,
If I didn't rain on her garden that was already blue.

Let me offer you my heartfelt candor,
This part of me that often stir these questions,
I began just like you who would not trust others,
Caring less and shutting, seemingly with all justified
reasons.

However, I feel I am best living around,
Those who are keen and those pretending about,
A sense of persona I culture as I dawdle the town,
Firstly, just let go of the perfect view of people and
most of all, your self-doubt.

Having faith is a subject of perception, in my view,
It's not about them but all about the attitude you permit,
I don't trust that no one is ever going to betray me,
I trust that I can handle it and to that I submit.

Short Poems

<u>***Decorated Heart***</u>

"Her aura is made of poetry, roses and galaxies", she
read,
Staring at the frequency of the words that resonates
with her vibration,
She picked her quill and continued the sentence.

"Her heart is decorated with fabrics, love and
landscapes,
And her soul is consumed by characters, adventures and
healing scars."

Soaring Wonderment

Every two weeks, my wonderment soars,
Did I learn? Did I reach?
Have I grown? What's in store?
Every muscle that was in grief,
Has it become a stepping stone?
For all the miles I still have to reap,
For I have been sowing my tired soul.

I'm rare

"I'm aware that I am a rare breed of woman."
I slept on otherwise for a long time before
I opened my eyes and put it in gear,
After untying the blindfold
That I didn't willingly wear.

"Love unconditionally and the world will become
gentle."
Ravel into the mystery of kindness
And let it unfold the true power
That the humanity beholds
For it will unleash the flock that is blind less.

Lonely Times

She used to think she has the most caring friends,
They are in a way, in the way they understand care.
She used to feel important enough to them to be sad if
they lost her,
But everyone's getting comfortable accepting loss if it's
too much to bear.

Why is it lonely if there's more than a billion people
around?
Is it that hard to find one that wouldn't make her scar
burn?
Or maybe it's hard because we aren't seeking true
company,
Just yet another opportunity to not feel unhappy or
worse numb.

<u>*Thoughts*</u>

Twirl around in that thought, unfold the latent.
For you shall find wholeness where you lost yourself.
Dunk from that thought, tighten the loose.
For the wholeness should enlighten not arrest.

Whole in the Lone

One step on a stone or one-stepping stone,
Lying on a cold hearth home.
Bring one to the whirling sandy loam,
And watch it ricochet back to your empty, dried dome.

Because things have a way of returning back home,
Whether its stones, you, or your memories in red zone,
Either you surrender or dance with that leprechaun,
That has nestled its name on that ricocheting stone.

But sometimes things don't really return back home,
They get lost, webbed, drown, or just disappear on its
own.
And sometimes it's good that they're gone,
For when you lose, you remember what really makes
you whole in the lone.

The Whisper and The Whisperer's Found

The hushed whisper is my favorite sound,
Let's you lean in to feel the warmth of every thought,
Digressing and tuning the strings between the whisperer
and the whisperer's found,
The conversation sang a song,
While they hummed to the chorus at every round.

If you get closer, you hear the pulsing beats,
That perfectly harmonizes with the rhythm inside the
cryptic lines,
And patches the pattern into a playful melody written in
the experimental sheets,
What started as a whisper echoed through space and
time,
To return to the receiver to shiver the spine waiting to
be remedied.

An Eerie Effervescent

She became an eerie effervescent,
For his love was left reticent,
He couldn't dare to tell her that his feelings were
decent,
And ended up searching bits of her in everyone else in
the end.

Slowly, he found that the world was shifting its
seasons,
In complete rhythm with his untenable reasons,
Sometimes these people enter the crevices of our
unhealed versions,
And repair what they didn't break from other unfinished
conversations.